T0006784

AXIS PARENT GUIDES SERIES

A Parent's Guide to Teen FOMO

A Parent's Guide to Influencers

A Parent's Guide to Instagram

A Parent's Guide to TikTok

A Parent's Guide to YouTube

A Parent's Guide to Teen Identity

A Parent's Guide to LGBTQ+ & Your Teen

A Parent's Guide to Body Positivity

A Parent's Guide to Eating Disorders

A Parent's Guide to Fear & Worry

A Parent's Guide to the Sex Talk

A Parent's Guide to Pornography

A Parent's Guide to Sexual Assault

A Parent's Guide to Suicide & Self-Harm
Prevention

A Parent's Guide to Depression & Anxiety

A Parent's Guide to Tough Conversations

A Parent's Guide to Cancel Culture

A Parent's Guide to Racism in the United States

A Parent's Guide to Walking through Grief

A Parent's Guide to Talking about Death

PARENT GUIDE BUNDLES

Parent Guides to Social Media

Parent Guides to Finding True Identity

Parent Guides to Mental & Sexual Health

Parent Guides to Connecting in Chaos

A PARENT'S GUIDE TO TOUGH CONVERSATIONS

A PARENT'S GUIDE TO

TOUGH CONVERS- ATIONS

Tyndale House Publishers
Carol Stream, Illinois

Visit Tyndale online at tyndale.com.

Visit Axis online at axis.org.

Tyndale and Tyndale's quill logo are registered trademarks of Tyndale House Ministries.

A Parent's Guide to Tough Conversations

Designed by Lindsey Bergsma

For information about special discounts for bulk purchases, please contact Tyndale House Publishers at csresponse@tyndale.com, or call 1-855-277-9400.

Library of Congress Cataloging-in-Publication Data

A catalog record for this book is available from the Library of Congress.

ISBN 978-1-4964-6774-4

Printed in the United States of America

29	28	27	26	25	24	23
7	6	5	4	3	2	1

Your kids will talk to you about things you talk to them about. Your kids won't talk to you about things you don't talk to them about.

CRAIG GROSS,
FOUNDER OF XXXCHURCH

CONTENTS

A LETTER FROM AXIS

Dear Reader,

We're Axis, and since 2007, we've been creating resources to help connect parents, teens, and Jesus in a disconnected world. We're a group of gospel-minded researchers, speakers, and content creators, and we're excited to bring you the best of what we've learned about making meaningful connections with the teens in your life.

This parent's guide is designed to help start a conversation. Our goal is to give you enough knowledge that you're able to ask your teen informed questions about their world. For each guide, we spend weeks reading, researching, and interviewing parents and teens in order to distill everything you need to know about the topic at hand. We encourage you to read the whole thing and then to use the questions we include to get the conversation going with your teen—and then to follow the conversation wherever it leads.

As Douglas Stone, Bruce Patton, and Sheila Heen point out in their book *Difficult Conversations*, "Changes in attitudes and behavior rarely come about because of arguments, facts, and attempts to persuade. How often do *you* change your values and beliefs—or whom you love or what you want in life—based on something someone tells you? And how likely are you to do so when the person who is trying to change you doesn't seem fully aware of the reasons you see things differently in the first place?"[1] For whatever reason, when we believe that others are trying to understand *our* point of view, our defenses usually go down, and we're more willing to listen to *their* point of view. The rising generation is no exception.

So we encourage you to ask questions, to listen, and then to share your heart with your teen. As we often say at Axis, discipleship happens where conversation happens.

Sincerely,
Your friends at Axis

---

[1] Douglas Stone, Bruce Patton, and Sheila Heen, *Difficult Conversations: How to Discuss What Matters Most*, rev. ed. (New York: Penguin Books, 2010), 137.

LIFE IS SCARY— WHICH IS WHY OUR KIDS NEED US TO TALK ABOUT IT.

ONE OF CHRISTY'S (NOT HER REAL NAME) earliest memories is her parents putting her to bed during a thunderstorm. She was scared of the thunder at first, but her parents talked to her about how neat the thunder was and how it showed God's awesome power. Christy believes that the fact she still sees thunderstorms as awe-inspiring is completely due to how her parents talked to her about them. If they had acted like storms were frightening, she most likely would have grown up hating them.

As parents, we have the ability to shape how our kids see topics that could be uncomfortable and scary. If we treat sex, for example, as embarrassing and taboo, our kids will most likely see it that way as well. They'll still be curious about it, but they'll also view it through a lens of shame and fear. However, if from the time our kids are young, we treat sex as something they can talk to us about, we will help them not to be afraid of it. More than that, we will set ourselves up as the main authority speaking into their lives about it, instead of leaving them to pop culture and their friends.

Bringing up tough conversations about subjects like sex, bullying, suicide, pornography, death, or school shootings is intimidating. We might want to do everything we can to avoid those conversations or to get out of them as fast as possible when they come up. It's understandable, but just as we wouldn't put our kids behind the wheel without any driver's training and hope it all turns out okay, we can't and shouldn't do the same with other skills—including coping, grieving, and standing up for themselves.

So rather than seeing these discussions as something to fear, we encourage you to think of them as valuable opportunities from our gracious God. Handled well, these conversations will allow you to influence your kids in important areas of life, as well as set the tone for the rest of their lives. Your willingness to be vulnerable will teach *them* to be vulnerable. It will teach them not to run away from difficult topics and situations and to confront their feelings and deal with them in healthy ways. Maybe best of all, it will strengthen your bonds with your children.

Rather than seeing these discussions as something to fear, we encourage you to think of them as valuable opportunities from our gracious God.

WHAT SHOULD I ADDRESS WHEN MY KIDS ARE YOUNG?

SEX AND PORNOGRAPHY

This is by far the most important conversation to begin when our kids are young. Culture starts the discussion about sex with our kids early and only increases its frequency from there. **We need to start talking to our kids about sex as soon as they're able to start talking.** This doesn't mean to go into graphic detail with little children, but it's crucial that we set ourselves up as the primary influencers for how our kids understand this part of life. What's more, it's a real possibility that our kids could be (or already have been) exposed to porn at a very young age. Approximately 10 percent of kids under the age of ten are exposed to porn,[1] and many put the *average* age of porn exposure at eleven years old. We also know people who discovered masturbation (which often carries a lot of confusion and shame) when they were quite young.

One man who is now thirty years old says his dad had the sex talk with him when he was thirteen or fourteen. Even though the dad included masturbation in that talk, it was at least five years too late for that (not to mention that he had already been exposed to porn). We might dread the thought of talking about these things with our kids, but it helps to consider the alternative. If we *don't* talk to them, it's highly likely that they'll be confused, ashamed, and secretive. If we *do* get over the embarrassment and fear and initiate these conversations, we'll be able to love, guide, and help our kids.

BULLYING

Bullying can happen to anyone, including adults, but it often starts when kids are young. If we don't address it, bullying could lead to a normalization of cruelty, mental health issues, or worse. Even

If we *do* get over the embarrassment and fear and initiate these conversations, we'll be able to love, guide, and help our kids.

if our kids don't participate in or suffer from bullying or cyberbullying yet, it's likely they'll see it happen to someone else at some point. They need guidance on what to do if they or someone they know is bullied.

DEATH

Raising the topic of death may be less urgent than talking about the previous two topics because it's hard to say when kids will have to deal with death up close. However, it's wise to prepare them for death *before* tragedy strikes, especially if there's a natural way to bring it up—for instance, if they see an animal die or hear about the death of someone who isn't close to them. This way, they will have some context for dealing with a more personal loss when it comes.

OTHER TOPICS

You know your children, your family, and your circumstances best, so if there's another tough topic (abortion, LGBTQ+ issues, smartphone habits, social media, divorce . . .) you think needs to be addressed, listen to that intuition. Again, there's a balance between preparing your kids and scaring them, so get advice from someone you trust or from a health professional if you're not sure when or how to talk about something.

There's a balance between preparing your kids and scaring them, so get advice from someone you trust or from a health professional if you're not sure when or how to talk about something.

HOW DO I INITIATE DIFFICULT CONVERSATIONS?

1. START BY LOVING YOUR KIDS WELL.

By far the most important steps you can take to make tough conversations easier are

1. Make it a habit to show you care about your kids by taking an interest in what they have to say and the things they enjoy.

2. As they grow up, make it part of your family culture to have open and ongoing conversations about difficult topics.

In other words, be proactive, not reactive. If you make it normal to talk about awkward subjects, resolve conflict with each other in healthy ways, and wrestle through difficult ideas, then it's much less likely that you'll be asking yourself, *How on earth do I bring up [insert topic* *here] with my teenager?* (Or worse, that you'll realize your kids have learned what to believe or how to act from other, less reputable places.)

God is our example for this way of approaching tough conversations. He's not afraid of confronting us with the truth, and He doesn't shrink back from difficult situations. He also loves us more than we could ever understand and demonstrated that by dying on the cross and giving us new life. He does not merely pay our debts; He walks with us through our lives, showing us mercy and carrying our burdens. First John 4:19 says the reason we love is because He first loved us. This principle applies not only to our relationship with God but also to our relationships with people. The old cliché "People don't care how much you know until they know how much you care" exists for a reason.

Your kids need to know you really care. Besides telling them you love them (which is very important!), take an active interest in the things they love, even if you think those interests are weird or off-putting. We spoke with many people who grew up loving all kinds of music. It would've meant the world to them if their parents had tried to understand why they loved the music they did, even though their parents may have hated that type of music.

2. BE CREATIVE AND INTENTIONAL.

If we wait for these conversations to happen naturally, we'll wait too long. So be on the lookout for ways to intentionally raise hard topics with your children. For example, you could use experiences from daily life, such as

- TV shows and movies
- what they're learning at school

- social media

- YouTube videos

- their friends

- billboards

- the news

- sermons

- the Bible

These are simply suggestions. Be imaginative and see what else you can come up with! **Something else that's helpful is if you and your spouse model how to have these conversations.** One couple we spoke with routinely discusses what they believe about certain difficult issues, and they do this *in front of their kids*. Not only do their kids overhear what their parents believe, but they also see first-hand the process of how to think through what *they* believe.

If we don't let shame about our pasts stop us from being vulnerable with our kids, God can use our personal failures to make a significant redemptive impact on them.

3. AVOID EUPHEMISMS.

This advice applies to anything we're uncomfortable talking about, whether that's body parts, sexual terms, or even death. Euphemisms imply that there is something to be afraid or ashamed of, and they open the door to confusion. Yes, there are appropriate times and places for talking and not talking about certain things. But if, for example, we use made-up words for *vagina* or *penis*, we're making it likely that our kids will be confused and embarrassed when they discover no one else uses those euphemisms. If we tell our kids that grandma went to "a better place," depending on how old they are, they might think she's still alive, just somewhere else. Let's love our kids enough to be honest with them.

4. REMEMBER THAT ALL KIDS ARE DIFFERENT.

Some kids will be more curious than others. We talked to one woman who never raised the topic of sex with her parents. She wasn't the type to be overly curious and ask a ton of questions. Her sister, on the other hand, was very curious. The only reason the woman found out what sex was is because she was there when her sister asked their mom about it. If one kid seems more reluctant to talk or never brings up a subject, don't assume that means you shouldn't discuss it. But remember, what worked for one child may not work for another.

5. DON'T ASSUME ANYTHING.

If your kids tell you they already know what sex is, don't breathe a sigh of relief and drop the subject. Remember, the whole goal is to be proactive in discipling your kids into God-honoring mentalities and perspectives. Your kids might have some wrong ideas about sex! One man we talked to said he got some very bizarre information from his friends when he was a boy. Plus, our culture defines many different acts as "sex." Even once your kids know what the basic sex act is, they still need your guidance on the multitude of issues related to sexuality.

6. APPROACH THESE CONVERSATIONS IN AGE-APPROPRIATE WAYS.

One mom we spoke with says that when her kids were growing up, she would answer difficult questions honestly no matter what age her kids were. However, she adjusted the level of detail she went into depending on their ages. Check out this article from Common Sense Media: https://www.commonsensemedia.org /articles/how-to-talk-to-kids-about -difficult-subjects.[2] It gives some helpful principles for how to frame conversations depending on how old your kids are.

7. PRAY AND LOOK FOR OPPORTUNITIES.

Frankly, praying and looking for opportunities are some of the best pieces of advice we can offer! Parenting requires so much wisdom because you face many circumstances where it's not clear which path is best. In such situations—which we all encounter, whether or not we're parents—we can and should bring our questions before the Lord, asking for wisdom and guidance.

One mom we talked to had an abortion before she got married and had kids. As her children were growing up, she believed it was important to share her past with them at some point, including how God had shown her grace and healed her. But how should she raise such an uncomfortable topic? And when should she bring it up? What she did was pray and look for opportunities. She

Besides telling them you love them (which is very important!), take an active interest in the things they love, even if you think those interests are weird or off-putting.

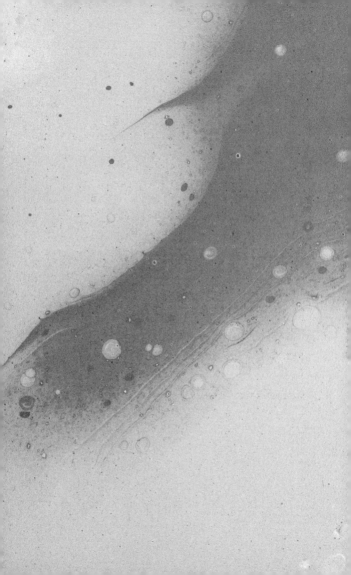

ended up sharing her story with each of her kids at different ages and for different reasons. One of her daughters went through trauma at a young age, so the mom shared her story with that daughter earlier than she shared it with her other children. If any of her kids were wrestling with sin in their lives, she saw that as an opportunity to tell her story and talk about how God was gracious to her. Living an authentic Christian life is crucial to helping your kids make good choices. **If we don't let shame about our pasts stop us from being vulnerable with our kids, God can use our personal failures to make a significant redemptive impact on them.**

WHAT ELSE SHOULD I KEEP IN MIND?

SOMETIMES THESE CONVERSATIONS will naturally arise from unexpected opportunities. But often you'll need to *deliberately* raise difficult subjects with your kids. Sex is the most obvious of these, but you might know that your kid is going through something specific and want to talk to him or her about it. Maybe someone in your family or a close friend of theirs has passed away, for example, and you feel the need to talk with your child about death. If you're unsure about where and how to begin, here are some things to think about:[3]

Consider the timing. Avoid times when you or your kids will be tired or stressed, and make sure you'll have enough time for the discussion instead of being rushed.

Consider the environment. Avoid places that are stressful and where you could be interrupted. If sitting across from each other at a table is going to be awkward, think about going on a walk so that you're doing an activity, out in nature, and not having to make eye contact the whole time. (Yes, sometimes too much eye contact can make an already-awkward conversation even more painful.) Maybe there are certain projects you enjoy doing with your kids. Starting hard conversations while working on something together can be a good idea since you'll both have a way to occupy yourselves instead of sitting in awkward silence. You'll be doing something you're already comfortable with, and you'll have a reason to stay in the room and therefore in the conversation.

Be strategic with how you start. You don't want to be too aggressive or so subtle that your kids don't know what you're talking about. You could start by saying you'd like their advice on a particular topic, but make sure you're being honest and not merely trying to find a way to start the discussion. Try to connect what you're talking about to something that's already happening in their lives—at school, for example. With younger kids, you could use a book to bring up the topic. Try to avoid just asking questions that have yes and no answers.

Be calm. Let them know you're not going to react in anger or shame them, no matter what. It's extremely important that you give yourself time to calm down so you don't have a discussion while grief or anger is running high. If you're not careful about this, you're basically guaranteed to say something you'll regret, as well as increase your kids' sense of shame, shutting them down. When the mom of one teenager caught him viewing porn, she started crying uncontrollably—an understandable reaction, but it just made him feel worse than he already did about what he'd done.

On the other hand, some parents we talked to accidentally read part of their daughter's journal (she'd left it out with the pages open) and discovered some pretty shocking language and disturbing behavior. They could have gotten upset with her for using the words she did and for not telling them what she was going through. Instead, they expressed how much they loved her and how concerned they were, which helped her open up to them.

If your kids raise a hard topic and you're not sure what to say or think, that's okay! Be honest with them and give yourself time to mull it over.

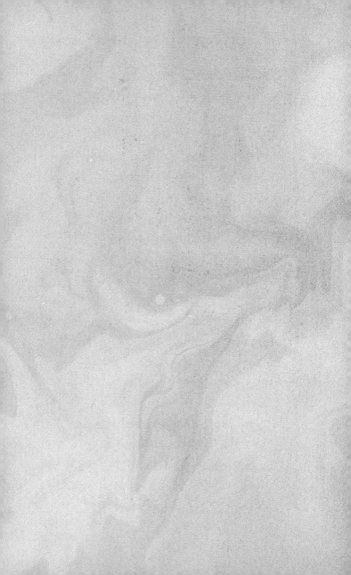

Listen well. Let your kids take as long as they need to answer, ask questions, and process. Don't interrupt them.

Be humble and willing to learn. One woman said that her parents weren't great at tough conversations because the way they communicated was not particularly compassionate, and they weren't willing to consider her point of view. As one grandmother we talked to points out, we've all experienced getting further down the road of life and seeing things differently. This can happen to any of us, so it's essential that we remain humble.

Have realistic expectations. Do your best *not* to idealize how it will go. (We've all run through conversations in our head, imagining a perfect ending, right?) Life is messy. If you're having the sex talk, expect that it will be weird. Why? Because it's a weird talk! Embrace that and don't be afraid. It's better for your kids to have an awkward conversation with you than to go elsewhere in search of answers.

Let them ask questions. Do what you can to anticipate the questions and responses your kids might have so you're better prepared to answer them.

Be honest. Tell them what you think, and be truthful if you don't understand. If your kid comes out to you as gay or trans, for instance, it's okay to be honest about how you feel. **But you must express that your love for them will never waver.** In the short film "Dear Church: I'm Gay," parents Brad and Robin Harper describe how their first response was to panic when their son Drew came out to them. But throughout the years that followed, they say that by far the most important thing they did was never cut off their relationship with him.[4]

If you need to take legal action based on what your kids have shared, let them know you're going to do that so they don't feel betrayed when you do. An example would be if they share that someone has sexually abused them. If your kids raise a hard topic and you're not sure what to say or think, that's okay! Be honest with them and give yourself time to mull it over—*but don't forget to have the conversation once you've had time to process*. You can also suggest that you and your kids find the answers to their questions together.

Get support, before or after these conversations. All of us need help from people we trust to make it through life's challenges. Consider sharing your situation and getting advice from mentors or friends. Other parents can also be an invaluable resource for you.

Think long-term. One reason tough conversations are, well, tough is because they are complex. *You can't adequately address a complicated topic in one conversation,* not to mention that your kids will keep changing and growing. Revisit these talks as time passes. It's also wise to let babysitters and anyone else who helps take care of your kids know how you'd like them to handle it if your kids ask them hard questions.

Give your kids space to process their feelings. If your kids are wrestling with serious pain or evil, don't expect them to magically be okay short-term. People need time to work through grief and suffering. Be there for them.

WHAT IF MY KIDS ARE OLDER BUT I HAVEN'T LAID THE GROUNDWORK FOR THESE CONVERSATIONS?

DON'T BEAT YOURSELF UP ABOUT IT. But also don't let it stop you from starting ASAP. It's *never* too late to start talking about the things that matter! It will probably be a hard battle, *but it's one you should fight*. Remember, it will be a lot harder to talk about difficult issues if you haven't built trust with your kids or set a precedent for having open dialogue, so you might need to start there first.

No matter how they act or what they say to you, your teens do care about what you think, and they do want you to care about what they care about. Apologize for how you've failed them, and explain that you want to know and love them and help them through difficult issues. Pursue them, even if they resist you. (What a beautiful way to make God's love more tangible and real!)

Some friends of ours recently went through training to be foster parents. One of the things they learned in their training was that the most important thing a foster kid needs is simply to be in a healthy, loving home. In the same way, more than your advice or instruction, *your kids need to know you love them*. It could be that this is what they need in order to stop acting out and start listening to you. It's not a magic bullet, though. You may not see any immediate results, but keep persevering.

More than your advice or instruction, *your kids need to know you love them.*

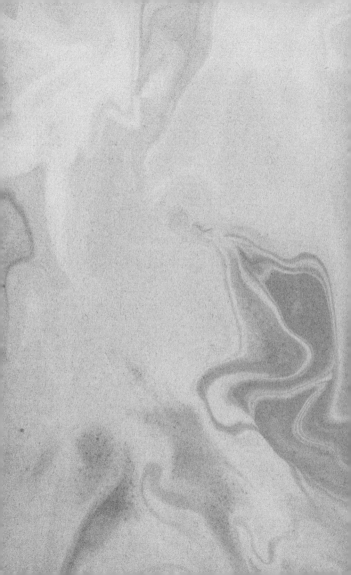

WHAT IF I MESS UP A CONVERSATION?

HAVE GRACE FOR YOURSELF! Apologizing goes a long way. And being humble enough to laugh at yourself does too. Whatever you do, don't give up or avoid these talks. You will have them imperfectly, and that's okay. Have them anyway. God uses imperfect people who are willing to follow Him. Pray, get advice from others, and persist. You'll get better the more you practice.

WHAT ARE SPECIFIC WAYS TO REACH MY GEN ZERS?

DEPENDING ON WHOM YOU ASK, members of Generation Z were born sometime from the mid- to late 1990s up until now. Also known as iGen, postmillennials, plurals, founders, and digital natives, Gen Z has grown up in a world dominated by the internet, smartphones, and social media. Needless to say, the presence of these technologies has impacted the methods by which they communicate, as well as the content they share.[5]

The best approaches for reaching Gen Z kids are those that leverage new technologies to their advantage, rather than those that avoid them altogether *or* those that rely solely on them. People are still people, no matter what generation they're in. We *all* need real, tangible human connection, no matter how technologically connected we are.

So how can we leverage technology to reach these digital natives? First, we must be willing to connect with our kids via their preferred methods. If they never pick up the phone when we call or listen to our voicemails, there could be a reason. One woman in her thirties realized that her youngest brother (now twenty-one) liked using Snapchat, so she got on Snapchat to connect with him better. This *began* their conversation by creating points of connection here and there, but she continued to use other means of communication to connect with him on deeper levels. So, by all means, talk to your kids using the technology they prefer. You could send silly Snaps to laugh with them and show them you care. You could message them on social media to ask if they want to hang out or have a face-to-face conversation later. *But*

The best approaches for reaching Gen Z kids are those that leverage new technologies to their advantage, rather than those that avoid them altogether *or* those that rely solely on them.

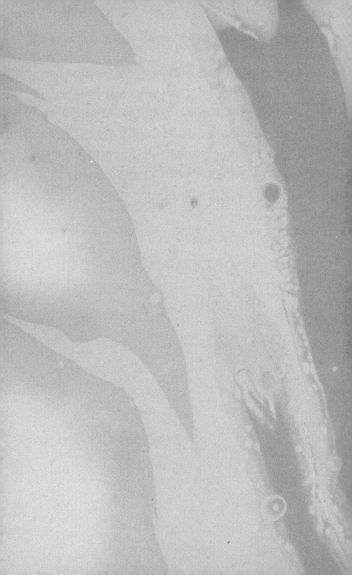

always have important conversations in person. Also, since many Gen Zers love watching videos on YouTube, it might be a good idea to watch a YouTube video together on the topic you want to bring up and discuss it with them afterward.[6]

ANYTHING ELSE TO KNOW?

GUESS WHAT? Tough conversations don't end when our kids grow up! One mom we spoke with had to confront her adult daughter because the daughter was being influenced by very subtle false teaching while she was serving on the mission field. Because the mom was providing financial support, she was concerned she'd be supporting a false gospel, so she and her husband had to talk with their daughter about it. The point is that your kids will still need your wisdom, support, and guidance even when they're grown. How you decide to have these conversations now will not only help them while they're young but also shape how you help them in the future.

Recognize that, at the end of the day, your kids will have to make their own choices. Maybe you're great at having these conversations. Maybe you bring them up frequently. At some point, your kids will have to bear the consequences of their own decisions. When one woman's son wanted to go to a certain college but wasn't willing to put in the work to get the scholarships he needed, his mom had to learn to let him fail. He ended up learning his lesson much more effectively as a result. He started working harder so that he was eventually able to transfer to the college he really wanted to attend. So it's important that we don't view tough conversations as the silver bullet that will solve all our problems, but rather as another tool in our toolbox for discipling our kids to love and follow God in every area of their lives.

Recognize that, at the end of the day, your kids will have to make their own choices.

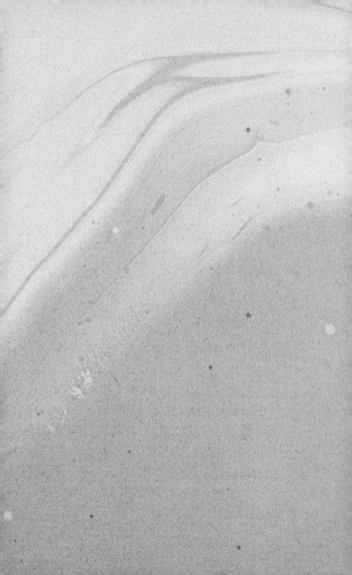

RECAP

- Rather than something to fear, tough conversations are opportunities for you to help your kids, disciple them, and strengthen your relationships with them.

- You need to start having certain conversations when your kids are very young.

- Be proactive, not reactive. Love your kids well, look for opportunities to start these discussions, and rely on the Holy Spirit.

- Beware of using euphemisms, treating all your kids the same, and making assumptions.

- There are a number of strategies for how to have these conversations well, but all require humility, wisdom, honesty, and love.

- Even if your kids are teens and you've only just realized the importance of tough conversations, start having them now. Never assume it's too late.

- Have these conversations early and often, and continue speaking into your kids' lives even after they become adults.

Even if your kids are teens and you've only just realized the importance of tough conversations, start having them now. Never assume it's too late.

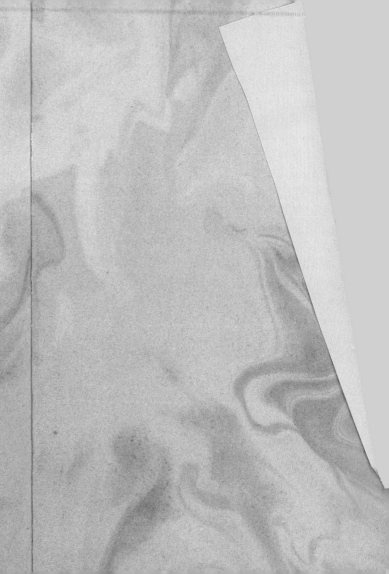

DISCUSSION QUESTIONS

1. Do you feel safe talking to me about anything? Why or why not?

2. If you were in trouble or had done something wrong, who would you talk to? Why?

3. How can I make you feel safer and more comfortable talking to me about anything, even things you know will upset me?

4. Is there anything you feel like you can't talk to me about right now? If so, what would it take for you to be willing to talk to me about that?

5. When I've brought up difficult topics with you in the past, what did I do well? What did I do poorly?

6. What topics do you wish we discussed more openly together?

7. What would help make awkward subjects feel less awkward?

8. What do you like or dislike about how your friends' parents handle difficult conversations with them?

9. Even when I need to have a disciplinary conversation with you, how can I better show you that I do it because I love you and want what's best for you?

FINAL
THOUGHTS

GOD IS A KIND AND LOVING FATHER who never stops loving us and who isn't afraid of anything we bring before Him. As His beloved children, let's show our children His love by intentionally discipling them in their daily lives *and* in the most painful and challenging aspects of their lives.

ADDITIONAL RESOURCES

1. Adriana Velez, "How to Tell Kids about Divorce in the Most Loving, Compassionate Way," Care.com, https://www.care.com/c/how-to-explain-divorce-to-kids/

2. Irina G., "What Losing My Pet Showed Me about the Power of Grief," Care.com, https://www.care.com/c/helping-kids-deal-with-the-loss-of-a-pet/

3. Nicole Schwarz, "How to Talk with Your Children about Difficult Topics," Imperfect Families, https://imperfectfamilies.com/how-to-talk-with-your-children-about-difficult-topics/

4. "Sibling Death and Childhood Traumatic Grief: Information for Families," National Child Traumatic Stress Network, https://www.nctsn.org/resources/sibling-death-and-childhood-traumatic-grief-information-families

5. "Addressing Grief: Tips for Teachers and Administrators," National Association of School Psychologists, https://www.nasponline.org/resources-and-publications/resources-and-podcasts

/school-safety-and-crisis/mental-health
-resources/addressing-grief/addressing
-grief-tips-for-teachers-and-administrators

6. US Department of Education, "Coping
   with the Death of a Student or Staff
   Member," *ERCM Express*, https://rems
   .ed.gov/docs/copingw_death
   _studentorstaff.pdf

7. David J. Schonfeld, "Talking with Children
   about Death," National Center for School
   Crisis and Bereavement, https://www
   .schoolcrisiscenter.org/wp-content
   /uploads/2017/05/Talking-with-Children
   -About-Death.pdf

8. Dougy Center, https://www.dougy.org/

NOTES

1. "The Detrimental Effects of Pornography on Small Children," Net Nanny, December 19, 2017, https://www.netnanny.com/blog/the -detrimental-effects-of-pornography-on -small-children/.

2. Caroline Knorr, "How to Talk to Kids about Difficult Subjects," Common Sense Media, March 12, 2020, https://www.commonsense media.org/articles/how-to-talk-to-kids-about -difficult-subjects.

3. "Talking about Difficult Topics," National Society for the Prevention of Cruelty to Children, accessed January 23, 2023, https://www .nspcc.org.uk/keeping-children-safe/support -for-parents/talking-about-difficult-topics/.

4. The Center for Faith, "Dear Church: I'm Gay," Vimeo, video, 20:38, August 25, 2017, https:// vimeo.com/231166638.

5. "Generation Z," Wikipedia, accessed January 23, 2023, https://en.wikipedia.org/wiki/Generation _Z#Date_and_age_range_definition.

6. Monica Anderson and Jingjing Jiang, "Teens, Social Media and Technology 2018," Pew Research Center, May 31, 2018, https://www.pewresearch.org/internet/2018/05/31/teens-social-media-technology-2018/.

PARENT GUIDES TO SOCIAL MEDIA
BY AXIS

It's common to feel lost in your teen's world. Let these be your go-to guides on social media, how it affects your teen, and how to begin an ongoing conversation about faith that matters.

BUNDLE THESE 5 BOOKS AND SAVE

DISCOVER MORE PARENT GUIDES, VIDEOS, AND AUDIOS AT AXIS.ORG

www.axis.org

CP1805